*"My love for you is etched in the book of eternity,*
*The stars call my name,*
*And your voice sings with me,*
*In our prayers that are poems,*
*That we together write…"*

~ Kevin Mooney
Excerpt from *"Kayleigh's Voice"*

Copyright 2019-2020 © All Rights Reserved.
Kayleigh Mickayla Mooney and Kevin Michael Mooney.

For any permissions, including to use or copy, in part or in whole, please contact **clemys@sbcglobal.net** or **kmmlaw12@gmail.com**.

978-0-578-65072-2

**Preamble: The Best of Me**

God, you have given my daughter, Kayleigh, and me the gift of writing. It is our obligation to fulfill that talent. And so we do. The methods have changed as she and I have adjusted and continue to adjust, alter, engage and blend. When a lag occurs in the channel, it is me who is lagging; tired, grief struck, walking forward through the first truth and living in the second truth.

Kayleigh, Babygirl, following the innocent and horrible car accident that stole your physical life at the age of fifteen, physically dying in my arms and in my voice, I am now your pen in this physical dimension; a channel for your words and your message and mission. Our writing styles merge like two rivers in these pages, one flowing from a brown brackish water basin and the other from crystal clear turquoise Exuma waters. Magically, when my waters merge with yours, my water clears up and takes on an aqua tone, as we write upon your bed together each night, plotting out our continuous journey.

One month prior to this accident that eviscerated our lives, I wrote a poem to you and your brother entitled, "The Best of Me," that I texted to you late one July night; a love song to my children and an admission that only through you and your brother do I find my truest potential. That notion continues unabated as I have learned how to be with both of my children in each child's respective and current body type and dimension. The second stanza remains my battle cry of freedom:

*"...I give you this light,*
*That flows from this soul,*
*It sparks lightning white,*
*In a heartbeat that glows,*
*Its streams fill with memories,*
*Of life's fields and roads,*
*And leads to your spirit,*
*Where the best of me grows..."*

You have consistently, daily, hourly, given me glimpses of Exuma Infinite, our Heaven, and our home. As I continue this path, with heartbreaking awareness and grief without you in your physical body, I know as well, with rejoicing glory that I get to be with you daily in your spiritual body of light. We have never been parted.

I have seen your amazing progressions in Exuma Infinite. I see that you have now given this island, that has emerged from your palms, a name; a name as perfectly wonderful as you, "Ceili's Cay." Subtle, dear Kayleigh, hilarious, fitting and so rebelliously Irish. You named an island after yourself in your Irish translation. Of course you did, my child.

# ULTRAVIOLET WAVES UPON
# AN AQUA OPAL SEA

## "On Awakening Every Day"

Kayleigh, dear daughter, as you know, Mommy and Daddy made your physical body, but we did not make your soul. God is the architect of your soul, infused with angelic immortality. That is God's sacred creation.

Your life is not your physical body, though it was once encased within that beautiful body, through which, in our human days, we facilitated our contact in the physical world. However, the true contact between us ignites, not from our human shells, but from our souls within those physical bodies, until it is not, through transition into a higher body of light; in essence, the soul becoming, stretching, expanding even bigger into that true body, a body of light; life elevated, continuously brightening into completeness.

I do not need to physically die to be with you; I am with you right now. And right now. And right now. Not without effort. Not without setbacks, yet with great measure and results when I feel you hold my hand; when I hear your voice in my right ear; when you confirm your presence by running your fingers over the crown of my head, lifting my hair gently and opening my spirit like a can opener makes light work of metal sheath.

Though we live in your daily presence and miracles, and it counterbalances excruciating daily pain, our broken hearts cry and seep and wail for our baby in her physical body. However, whether you are in your physical body or spiritual body, you are still Kayleigh; you are still the same kid. If I cannot have you in your physical body, which I no longer can, I am going to do everything in my power, everything I can, to be with you in your spiritual body. I awaken each day with the full intention to blend with you; to lift to a higher vibration so I can be present and effective for both of our children, though you and your brother are now in two different body types; infusing myself into your light, joining you as you unveil your next miracle to me.

## "Squinting into the Ultraviolet"

The consequence of human,
Blinded before birth,
Stripped of intuition,
And eyes devoid of worth,
The lens blocks these wavelengths,
The cornea conspires,
And redacts the information,
That flows through its wire;

Encased in this human,
A spirit presses outward at the flesh,
Spending a lifetime,
Attempting to disrobe this organic vest...

...In the cage of this carnival,
We cannot even adapt,
And so the ultraviolet light,
Goes unobserved and streaming passed;

And here she is dancing,
A spotlight burning bright,
She pirouettes and the galaxies spin,
In her body of light,
I sense, feel and hear her,
For I refuse this conditional life,
And puncture the skins of my humanity,
And squint into the ultraviolet light;

Overriding the mechanics,
The user manual of the eyes,
I see her sparkle in my vision,
As I collapse the great divide...

...Your father is burning down the night,
And with my soul finding new sight,
And seeing a glimpse of the beach on which you live...

...Gives me hope in this new life...

**"Signs"**

As subtle as a hurricane is to the wind,
This one knows the channels where the veil is thin,
She throws the silver glitter, sparked gold and green,
In hopes his soul will see what the eyes fail in dreams -

And vigilance, its own reward,
Mark the find where her spirit soared,
Riddles, speak in tongues to the seeker's ear,
He feels the words when he cannot hear...

...And purple ribbons tied to delicate trees,
Dance among the flora and the rainbow leaves,
They line the path through thickets and stones,
In hopes her father finds his way back home...

...Pink Saturn, it breathes and rings overflow,
Novas, pulsing orange with transient glow,
A million crystals in the sky path blaze,
Just to catch attention to his wayward gaze...

...And then he sees - and then he felt it,
The signs so plentiful he cannot help it,
She praises him for each tiny gain,
In her way - as subtle as a hurricane!

**"Audience"**

And tumble, child, dressed in princess bows,
And made up face with lipstick and eye shadow,
You create an air of ambiance,
An ambient light for an audience,
You sit your father to the side in a chair,
Away from the space where the rug is clear,
And laugh and roll and throw yourself,
From your bed as our hearts melt...

...Yes, aware and awake I was,
As I always shall be,
Knowing the value of my audience,
I cheer you on and I become in your eyes,
A light like one million fireflies...

...Erupts.

**"In the Ministry of Your Light"**

So many the months in these preparations...

...Emerge from the womb, an entrance awaits,
At the start of the engine, at the edge of these new gates,
Burst into vocals streaming loudly clear,
Now that the lungs have filled with first air,
Gasp and gulp and God has delivered you,
You have now for five seconds entertained,
This reality set,
This human plain...

...And you grow and you grow day after day with that smile on your face...

...Your father, he knows the moment he is chasing after,
With fluttering heart and flittering laughter,
He shows you the stars and the grasses and the night and the moon,
And the birds and the salamanders and the way the caterpillar swoons,
Up through each and every year,
For he is in love with you,
He is in love with you...

...From that first breath until the shock of the last,
When the accident happened it was he who was there as you passed,
As he cradled your light with words and his presence,
And his fifteen year old child was altered in essence,
In that last breath,
In that premature physical death...

...And he loves you so,
And he grieves you so,
And he needs you so abundantly,
And you are in love with him,
You are so in love with him,
Reaching across this vapor veil,
Transparent and paper thin;

And he hears your voice,
And he feels your grace,
And he sees somehow,
The sparkles that light up your face,
And it breathes into him,
A higher, higher faith...

...For he knows you're here,
There beside him now,
Cradling him in the ministry of your light...

**"God, Into Yours..."**

...And God, wise and gracious, a Father most grand,
Took my daughter by her youthful hand,
Weeping for the accident that caused her physical death,
And like a great Father, he collapsed to his knees and into his hands,
Wept,
For she is His child,
For she is one of His favorite souls,
For she is incorruptible love,
In a spirit alive in a light body glow,
And He promised as He took my hand,
If I was willing to behold,
He would permit her constant guardian presence,
And turn this tragedy into gold...

"...And my God, into Your hands, as I calculate this toll,
My God, into Yours I commend my child's soul..."

**"Fatigue"**

Fatigue it wrestles with unrest,
Like pollen scratches throat and chest,
The blurry eyed, they poach their sight,
Just to steal some sleep at night;

But not for me - the ceiling boasts my gaze,
Enslaved by chains of broken days,
I blink the eyes and hours trace,
Darkened tender circles deep in quickly aging face;

While mind drools on in droning lull,
You shine like ocean moon when full,
You spread from fingers - swirl in waves,
The silver songs of glitter praise,
In prayer and meditation raise,
An elevation spirit claimed,
You live within your light of life,
Flesh of light and full moon bright...

**"Walking on Mars"**

Spread through the vigil of veritable night,
The seeds of sunrise sprout in blaze of first flailing light,
They spring from your palms and spread like a green sea of life;

You hold the words that flesh in this song,
You know the world has done us a wrong,
A wrong for which forgiveness is barred,
A horrible accident and now, here we are...

...I spun the wheels to turn back the time,
Held my breath to hear the meaning divine,
I stared at the trees until their faces of leaves fell upon me;

I took an audience with our beautiful Lord,
Peppered Him with questions like I was swinging a sword,
I fell to my knees and lashed at Him for responding;

I have screamed - I have cried,
Thrown a spear down its throat,
Tied off its venom with a snare and a rope,
And slept in its vomit like a blanket of moons and of stars;

I have died nearly one thousand deaths,
In each cresting peak of each painful breath,
Wept in the company of loneliness like I was walking on Mars...

...Yet this path continues until these eyes come to rest,
As I walk the red planet with medals pinned to my chest,
For I am a warrior with laurels from campaigns and conquest;

Though this is not true it's not far from the truth,
For I am a warrior in what I pursue,
A Daddy, in grieving, reaching across just to touch you.

## "The Pain That Lies Beneath"

If the midnight was blood and the darkness my veins,
There are moments so grievous,
No amount of morning can relieve this pain,
But for the grace of the moon,
No matter crescent or full,
As I swallow the waves,
I dream the consequence of its pull...

...Drifting into another new day,
The first thought always upon me,
Before my first full breath awake...

...My daughter has been physically killed,
The scabbard of my soul, it screams,
As the light of my spirit shakes,
In the dereliction of a father's grief,
Before the body rises,
While my feet are still asleep,
I am quite aware...

...Of the pain that lies beneath.

**"Writhe the Wraiths of Eyes"**

Gloom the starch that dried the night sticky,
Gloom the dark that swallowed light thickly,
It seeped out from the emotional turmoil,
And caught on fire in a temperament's boil,
And exploded like a meteor,
Uncomfortably,
That blew a hole a mile wide,
And set a forest ablaze,
As the tempest lit up this sky...

...Frenetic in this burn...

...Behold this wraith that writhes behind these eyes.

### "Fear"

It ravaged and swallowed stars,
Cutting a swath through the air,
Leaving ploughed trails of scars,
Scattered in the nebula atmosphere,
Where black holes feast,
And black holes, never satisfied, find themselves deceased;

This consistent sepsis of soul slaying grief,
This consistent essence of soul preying thief,
This consistent presence of low grade fear,
It is like itself the air,
The house guest that both the heart and lungs share;

It is so omnipresent that it has little known effect,
It is so aggravating it has permission to nest,
It is so concentrated that it's levity compressed,
Permitting no light to penetrate the chest,
Where the black holes feast,
Like fire and dry trees,
Dropping flaming leaves...

...A forest lay extinct.

**"The Return of the Hyena"**

Of triggers and frayed,
And shaking afraid,
I stare at the borders and corners,
Searching for spot to escape,
Studying my way out…

…There is no way out…

…Circling this metal box,
Covered in Pandora's pox,
My paws and claws click on the floor,
Circling the cage…

…One thousand times more…

…Leaving trails of blood and emotion,
Grief and devotion,
Scars of worship and wounds of grace,
Line this hyena's traumatized face,
Walking in circles,
Entrapped within circles,
I walk…

…Dream of the Stars that breathe on the glass of the sea…

## "Like This"

It rains down from the atmosphere,
It's fire tail, spiritless,
It aims down the barrel of fear,
Even if you've done your best,
And unleashes a raw velocity…

…Catch this meteor in the chest.

**"When Grief Stalks the Land"**

Sometimes like a tank ploughing through the front door,
Mostly though, more subtly, like a snake slithers on the floor -

The grief slips in like a quiet thief,
Into the hallways of disbelief,
Searching for the secret to sanctuary,
Pulled out from under your soul's feet,
Ever cunning and very discreet,
It sets off no alarm bells,
It surveys the street,
From the safety of the darkness of a hedgerow,
Waiting for its opportunity,
And it will come,
And it will come,
For he is patient, he is grief,
He has hidden tricks coiled in his sleeve,
And a den of laurels and trophies,
From those whom he's deceived,
From those whom he's deceived...

**"How Did I Get Here"**

I stumbled out from a flash of trauma,
Deposited on a desolate road,
On the whereabouts of the unknown,
From where I was - now so very far,
As far away as me waving up at bright stars,
To try to close the gap in the air,
And not truly comprehending…

…How did I get here?

Deposited on another planet,
Dropped upon its stony surface,
With no map and no reconnaissance,
And with no valid purpose,
I scream and my voice cowls the wind,
How, oh Lord…

…How did I get here?

And once upon this jagged land,
Where promise and hope are slain,
There is nothing but a hard road,
For the remainder of my days,
Reminiscing of the happy times,
And the love and lives we shared,
Wishing I could unwind time,
To wish me out of today,
And the torture present here.

## "Cherry Blossoms on a Crooked Tree"

There are scars like cherry blossoms on a crooked tree,
That sway to the melody of a frantic breeze,
Yet in its song the earth's ear bends,
Knowing we will rise again,
Knowing we will rise again;

The sun sparkles in the recesses of our souls,
And flutters captured in darker folds,
But bruises fade though woundings do not mend,
And though no healing comes,
I know that we will rise again,
I know that we will rise again.

**"Visible Life"**

We are enslaved by the mirage of visible light,
Within the spectrum of perception of the limits of the human eye,
We cage in our existence,
Though true life defines our boundaries,
And with constant persistence,
It crosses our dimensions to let us know,
Even if in whisper that true life is hereby visible to the aided eyes,
Invested with bodily natural form,
This instantiation too abstract to the one dimensional person,
Who simply see the human species' leather uniform;

I can catch in the lowest webbing of my human energy field,
So tethered to my organic cells in this physical atmosphere,
Where very little higher engagement bares a yield,
Yes, taste this bread through the pallet of my soul;

Esoterically believing,
Such a small group who truly understands,
Evidence dictates otherwise,
Yet the fulcrum burns the sweat away,
Like the sun melts humidity bands,
Manifesting conspiracy to deny the path of presence,
For the worlds converge as one,
Unless we rely on visible light,
Like staring at the sun…

…So blinded we have all become.

**"Mask"**

Pursue the mask and fate may bate the nascent pain,
Fueling hurricanes with barbed wire and spiral flames,
That lick the metal into liquid,
Within the heart that can't keep pace,
And breed the torture like fields plowed with rusty nails,
That etch their claws that rake their trenches into the fleshy face,
Until the man cannot find himself,
Not at all…

…Not a trace.

**"Exuma Sunrise"**

As with the promise,
Ever made,
Arching upward from marble waves,
Shrouded in scents of pastel shades,
Its aura dressed in morning's stains,
That bathes the world with light.

**"Soulfulness"**

Where, alight, the waters glisten,
Sparking rainbows in the cresting flow,
And the early arching sun spreads its golden blanket,
Brightly aglow,
It is here at the seaside,
Where I look for your soul,
And find you waiting patiently for me,
In this lovely place…

…Behold.

**"Please"**

Please, if you can summon your voice,
Louder than my mind's noise,
It would help me in my current state,
As I punch and push and pirouette through barricades;

Please, if you can drum up an echo to chase down the wind,
And ring your song in the wind chimes to wash out chagrin,
It would relieve at least some of this thieving weight;

And all the sounds of emptiness,
They bed themselves into the firmament,
Across the fields where the flocks of grief release,
I scream your name, compelled, and to my knees...

...Please, of Lord, please.

**"A Spirit in its Human Skins"**

And though, the limitations vex my desire,
I cross the wilderness and slog through its mire,
Cursed on this plain with matter and time,
Within these skins, and a human mind,
I elevate, though dust clouds strum,
Like buffalo hooves by the millions run,
I cry until my laughter comes,
And glistens, waxed like midday sun.

**"Every Century in Every Second"**

A mirage of separation,
A pitiless divide,
It rages over the shoulders of my mountains,
Like a hurricane rips the trees from its sides,
It ranges like an epidemic,
And rushes downward like a landslide,
The wheels of time in a century,
In every second hides.

## "Slainte, Kakes"

Am I feared abandoned,
Here on the lost frontier of the spiral arm of a lonely galaxy,
Filled with space debris and dimming stars and heavy metals,
While you call to me from the star forming regions of Heaven,
Rich with nebula light and fluorescent crystal life,
A compass for my heart,
On the outskirts of grief,
Your voice calls through my empty night…

…Like fast radio bursts,
Though as frequent as my breath,
Are we light years apart,
Are we light years away,
Since your physical death…

…From each other…

…But the dialect is sometimes magically peculiar,
Yet always familiar,
You have learned one thousand languages and use them in fusion,
Mixing syllables and sounds into a delicate and beautiful orchestra,
While you touch my hair,
While you literally, gently touch my hair…

…Running slow circles around my crown,
As if you are lifting the edges of my aura,
And radiating my skin with sound,
And the connection that I grieved was lost,
Once again is found,
For we are eternity itself,
In this pink cord of light we are bound.

**"In Many Forms"**

Is not snowflake water ice,
Spiked in crystals - guide its flight,
From the fields of clouds,
Spiral into a distance,
Where the ground, alive and white,
Catches snowflake - catch alight,
From the hand of God release,
Into this Kingdom...

...No, not to worry, not to fear,
There is a revolution, gathers here,
Here amongst the snowdrifts,
Here amongst the frozen sea,
Rejoice,
Rejoice,
Tomorrow's drinking water...

...Breathes.

## "Behind These Green Eyes"

I may smile in a greeting,
I may laugh, seemingly engaged,
I may wax and be entertaining,
But you do not see this cage,
It holds a panicked hyena,
That circles a metal box with rage,
For my perfectly happy and healthy daughter,
Has been physically killed,
At fifteen years of age!

The world with its current events,
And it's headlines and its gate,
Only those who similarly suffer,
Can understand this life sentence and its cruel fate…

…And these green eyes hold videos on replay,
While the vigilant summer birds clung to branches,
Hunkered silently, vigilantly in the trees above,
In the canopies of a Sycamore,
While the leaves turned red and blue,
From the harsh flashing lights of the vehicles of the first responders,
Addressing you below…

…Your father on his knees,
Having just held you as you took your last physical breath,
And, into and in through his light, released…

…The angels lay thousands of wreaths of light,
In every treetop and telephone pole,
On every wire, on every wisp of air,
With strings of stars and bushels of galaxies laid at your side,
Like blankets weaved into a universal ball of light,
That held us in that moment,
To comfort you in transition,
As they played the music of one thousand violins,
In reverence for you.

## "Solar Sea"

If every salt crystal was a planet,
And every wave that crests a galaxy,
It would still not contain enough light,
To match your energy;

If every water droplet was a moon,
And every tidal surge a solar sea,
It would still not portray the magnitude,
Of the love you have for me.

**"Resonance of Light"**

In a blinding flash, the tone of which is so bright,
It crashes through the barrier of sound,
And vibrates in resonance,
And vaccinates between the miraculous and the profound,
Leaving a fingerprint of her lovely voice,
Unrestricted, unbound,
For when light resonates across the dimensions,
It makes this humming sound,
That vibrates skin with spirit tones,
And bridges communication,
Between two loving souls.

## "Where the Turquoise Waters Rise"

The aqua, it's lightning, rakes the salt from the shoal,
Oh dear Mother Nature, is your bounty not full,
Dream of a landscape not fit for human eyes,
Land on a dreamscape where the electric ocean...

...And the sandbars collide,
A tongue of eternity,
Stretches out from island's side,
We walk crystal white sands,
Where the turquoise waters rise -

The hum in the ocean, alive, green and icy blue,
It radiates like fire light escapes from the moon,
The artist, she chances a white golden hue,
And brushes the face of my canvas...

...With the love of a mother this child has assumed,
Painting with oils the shades of Exuma,
A spectrum I cannot see with my eyes,
An ethereal eternity that binds our lives,
Please be patient, for there are times...

...I cannot have my ear to the door of Heaven twenty four/seven,
I cannot twenty four hours a day be pressed to the gates of Heaven...

...But I try...

**"Astral Traveling"**

And atop a mountain of green gems and jewels,
I sat in the clouds on an emerald stool,
The golden light sparkling, flow into crystalline pools,
That lay a mile below the mist in waters mystic and cool;

The sky deep and flexing in an indigo rash,
Sing with purple vibrations where the colors contrast,
Like a sea of galaxies wearing nebula mask,
I walked the stars on the spines of their backs;

And how did I get here - when there is no road,
How can a man fly through dimensional folds,
But for this angel and her eternal soul,
She took me by the hands and told me, "let's go!"

Her golden hair blew back and caressed my face,
As I lay across her shoulders and traveled through space,
She pointed to the planets and supernova waves,
She held my hands around her and professed to me thanks -

For being her father and trusting her light,
And traveling, though tethered, to my physical life,
We ranged through, together, many possible sights,
To visit again when the timing was right;

And then as our meditation loosened and ebbed,
And I released a final, calming, guttural breath,
She opened my eyes and kissed my forehead,
And brought me back - sitting here on her bed.

## "Today"

Oliva Sayana - shattered of bone,
Like a butterfly is crushed by stone,
Its pieces dance in the waves,
Across the range of sea graves,
Where the dust of their lives,
Settle into the beach's changing face;

She picks up my scarred and torn shell,
Brushes off the scorched marks from the fires of hell,
And throws me on her back,
Nearly lifeless, bewitched of fact,
My wounded frame, my wounded heart, my wounded soul,
And walked across the debris field of my life,
With only one goal...

...To safely guide me home.

**"Fingerprints from Heaven"**

And here the box of space and time confines,
The human condition and the human mind,
Fault and fury and folly and faith,
Rattle like nails in a metal cage;

And then the moonlight strikes the glass,
And symbols rise and sparkles dance,
Adorned across the window plain,
fingerprints from Heaven's domain;

And as dimensions merge through each other,
In that cross section we embrace one another,
For long the love it grows with grace,
And lives beyond all time and space;

And then the wind, it kiss the glass,
Her voice, it's strength, through window pass,
We laugh amongst the lush green yield,
That grows within...

...Our endless fields...

# A BODY INCARNATE OF STARS

**"A Glass of Fruit and Sugar Cane"**

Lime and lemon and sugar cane,
Iced and fresh with tea leaves strained,
A splash of mint, a hint of rain,
A glass of sun that washed the veins,
And cooled the skin, as tension wanes,
A glass of fruit and sugar cane...

...And back into the world again.

**"Celebrate"**

When my soul trembles,
(And my soul trembles),
And the fear causes my frame to shake,
I turn back to your smiling face,
My little girl,
My sweet Kayleigh Kakes,
And seize your example,
And grasp to this faith -

What is it that I cannot do,
When I think,
That my daughter, bristling with courage,
And caught in an innocent accident,
Climbed the mountaintop and stared into the silent sun,
And holds the hand of the Mighty One,
The Mighty One...

...How proud, my child, am I,
For you, of the two of us...

...Are truly alive.

## "This Is My Classroom"

Others may point up to a cold northern sky,
But we hold the southern coast in our eyes,
breathe thin lines of white smoke as the waves break at night,
In the shallows;

When deep in my sleep, these days, I meet you there,
As we laugh and we walk and the love that we share,
Illuminates the beachfront like full Supermoon, casting shadows,
As bright as the daylight is bending;

This is my classroom - my lessons of light,
These are the miracles that present in my life,
I'm watching - I'm hearing - the instinct is clearing,
The aching deep fog in my soul;

And you show your father the heat of the glow,
That melts off the icecaps and desolate snow,
That collected in corners in times when the light, seeming low,
Seems to miss me;

You lift my head up - you reset my feet,
You remind me that life didn't end in the street,
The accident came and released you into heavenly life,
Which is higher,
Than the observable multiverse is old;

I Float and traverse the abundant sky gardens,
In capsules of my tears,
Propelled into silent sobbing,
Draped in yellow spice in periwinkle clouds,
Drifting over the cays of Bahamas,
Until I open my eyes and press my feet again,
Into this earthly firmament.

### "My Children's Grace"

It is where the silky rainbows merge,
Where warm, sparkling waters converge,
Where one million blazing shades of brass gold,
Flow like blinding rivers aglow…

…For my children…

…It is the ocean fields of stars,
Indigo beacons in an endless heart,
It is carved in the softer features of my face,
When I live within my children's grace…

…That bare me forth like two North Stars,
That dance like Neptune's Thalassa and Naiad,
In an orbital resonance of faith.

**"If The Tables Were Turned"**

I would spread my light and love around you,
It would spark against your aura,
It would flood through the sacred chambers of your soul,
In a way that you would always know,
Your Daddy is with you,
And speaks with truth,
Your Daddy is with you,
I would wrap my arms around your grieving,
I would bring you gold to counter the thieving,
And lay it on the soil on which your feet would pass…

…If the tables were turned,
I would do as you would need and as you would ask…

…"So, Daddy, I ask,
And remember when you feel subdued,
Since the tables are turned the other way,
Why would you think I would not do…

…The same for you?"

**"Now Time is Slow"**

To watch for signs of the clock erode,
Like watching a mountain collapse stone by stone,
The minutes are lengthy and wrong,
Each a century in a second long...

...Now, now that time is slow...

**"One Second"**

If the world - if it could give me just one glance,
One second - one flash - one chance,
To hold you for just one moment again,
In exchange,
I would forfeit a thousand lives;

I see emblazoned in the wind - your lovely face,
Each day the tears flow,
When came that last physical embrace,
So long ago - yet not so long ago,
And sometimes the tears like knives,
They pool in the back of the eyes,
They do not release - they cannot release,
Encased behind this glass for forever.

## "The Dangerous Power in the Powerlessness"

I want to scream until my skin, in the vibration, sheds,
I want to rip the skin off of this life,
I want to rip the veil down shred by shred,
I want to throw caution to the wind,
And run headlong into the light…

…The powerlessness is so powerful it has the propensity to kill…

…I want to live as I had lived,
And I cannot,
Prior to the greatest pain that this life could give,
We are, as we hold, larger than this world,
We are, and your soul, my little girl,
Sets out the path for this heavenly road,
To walk us through these days,
While walking us home,
Yet the breathless moments that come,
In the depths of the powerlessness,
When the danger tolls…

…I dig in the feet and remember my promise,
To live, truly live, while I live on this tactile road,
For it is the only way I can hear your voice,
The voice that leads me home.

**"A Skiff upon the Ocean (Timelessness)"**

A skiff, pounded against progressions of waves,
Crossing this lifetime of joy and chagrin,
Painted one hundred times to keep the appearance of sheen,
Now pocked with thick, peeling, jagged alligator skins...

...I sail...

...One day at a time until eternity,
When the soul amasses maturity,
When the linear becomes remind-less-ness,
And time merges into timelessness...

...She awaits my passage on Ceili Cay,
Where there is no lull that comes and goes,
With only heights and never lows,
For there, escaped of space and time,
The soul it breathes and lives and shines;

I row, propelled with the fuel of love for your mother,
And brother,
And you,
I rest, and sleep, and ache, and cry, and balk, and continue;

No space nor time - nor accident's untimely rhythm,
Can long bar the walls or cage us with its prison,
For the four of us - as the centuries have told,
Exchange the human shell with an embodiment of gold,
And in this particular case,
We have together crossed the space divide,
We have conquered death itself...

...For we are wide awake,
Crowning the defiance of the temporary shell of humanity,
Invested by the power of God.

## "Luminous"

All life is light bearing,
All life may propagate light,
Invoking the ancients through tongues of thought,
A freshly born baby is equipped with new life,
Filling in this empty space,
With a flame that ignites a new born face;

Flakes of shedding light bristle at the darkness,
A soul is forever luminiferous,
No vacuum exists in which love is apparent,
Invisible to the eye, infinite and tangible,
Nor physical skins hold its presence but briefly,
Where cocoon opens to a new morning,
Like a room filled with thousands of candle flames alight…

…In a cauldron of waves, swirls of sunrise, eddy,
Many humans, unevolved, unawake, may not be ready,
Derelict in their spiritual health,
Flow the whirlpool into an apparition of life itself,
Comes to them and they deny themselves gold,
Denying themselves the higher nature of their souls,
But not us…

…Not us.

## "I Will Not Fail You"

The threads, exhausted, fray the edges of this day,
As the paint along the window panes flakes,
And the mind loosens in the mounting chaos of dismay,
Yet I promise this and hold its truth,
My Darling, your Daddy will rise again,
Through the grief and it's haze,
I will never fail you;

I lay across your bed - we write together new songs,
With a bucket of moonstones in my palms,
And the Moon hanging like a beacon of hope,
Blinking in the canopies,
As the wind dances in the summer trees,
This is our time to pull our way through,
My Darling, with a rope of one from strands of two,
Your Daddy will rise again,
I will never fail you.

## "The Opal Glow Upon the Sea"

Pulling the tides that rise in these eyes,
Tears like tiny waves,
Crash and disengage,
And recede into the cascading grind…

…Spring green scents spin from the color wheel…

…Mesmerized by mystic torch,
Blazing in the night, this night's sky,
Opal with a crystal lunar glow,
Opaque and orange and blue and bold,
The power it emanates,
The gradient it throws…

…I see you there in long white gowns,
Threaded with wisdom and peace,
Walking upon an ancient powder sand,
Along an indescribable stretch of beach…

…Its water, light minty bluish tints of whitish seafoam spray.

**"Untether"**

Untie yourself from this listless ground,
Where only a fraction of life may be found;

Amidst the lowest vibrations a soul can absorb,
Untether from the confines of this earthly floor;

And lift your life of love and live this love of light,
When you unleash the passion in your spirit core;

There is time now while you are still in human form,
To touch the highest levels before crossing through that door.

## "Divinity Eyes"

Heartache that owns no description,
It is impossible to convey...

...I long to be captive in the wisdom of your gaze,
To look upon the contours of your beautiful face,
To divine your emotion and guide your teenage days,
My child...

...Your eyes - in photos, videos, daydreams and memories,
They radiate like sparkling fields of aquamarine,
Sea sky sunset washed in indigo hue,
Quartz dipped in sunrise emitting a morning's blue,
I have always seen this beauty in you,
My Love...

...And I propel myself towards you,
In meditation this is clear,
As I lift myself higher,
My skiff banging violently through the waves,
I shatter the ceiling of this earthly sphere,
I lock my vision directly into your eyes,
Gazing back to me with the mystery of pride,
Knowing that, though I am encased within this human state,
I search endlessly to punch a hole through to the other side,
To band soul to soul,
To hold my physically deceased child,
(While I hug your brother close),
To find peace in that place,
Where the voice in your sapphire eyes,
Like warm and lovely arms,
Cradle me,
And I find rest...

**"Kayleigh Stones"**

Malachite stones,
Emerald bones,
Scattered jewels, bold and green,
They blanket the beach,
Strewn among golden beads,
Water gems from the morning rains,
Dewdrops and candy dots,
Catching light as the sun melts the cloud,
Calling light as the wind calls your name,
Your promise to me as we walk this plain,
You have never left,
You will never leave…

…Your love is the fire of the deep blue sea,
That polishes golden stones,
That light up my soul for Eternity…

**"Sleeper Still Searching"**

In the muddy crux and quagmire of a failed meditation,
Where I missed the ether train for an hour's vacation,
I stand like a bystander watching empty tracks,
Not knowing that the window of opportunity has already passed...

...Sleeper, sleep evades your sleepy eyes,
Tugging on the corners of a winter's icy sky,
Outside the streetlights glisten to a swirling wisp of snowflakes,
And with three blankets warm you should easily aqueous;

You study the noises of the boiler with its clanging and echo,
You pass your eyes on window panes that frame the branches,
With wispy dunes of frozen snow,
Yet still you struggle, Sleeper...

And fail to crawl within its dreamy folds...

...For hours and hours,
Until there is no strength left to withhold.

**"Purple Dreams"**

The heart is soothed with lacy lavender valleys,
That cradle immortal love,
It erupts from the center in a flowing radiant fountain,
And bursts outward and upward,
Like amethyst flowers erupt from volcanic mountain,
Spreading millions of purple petals across the grass,
And floating in the streams,
That illuminate at the edges with a diamond flash,
Bright white and orchid green,
She spins her fingers gently in the waters,
That ripple off into my dreams,
And kisses her Daddy's forehead,
With the creation of these scenes,
A perfect paradise that glows endlessly beneath her feet,
Into which, hand in hand, she guides me, though I sleep.

## "Songs of a Beach Wind"

A wind caught dancing in the bending shafts,
Sea oats rooted in sand and crab grass,
Like silky petals abloom and pastel scented,
Flowing like faint rainbows - calm, iridescent,
Through a heavy air amidst a thunder heat,
We hear its chorus and harmonics of peace,
That passes from the ears and the eyes towards the soul,
And vanquishes stress once immersed in its fold.

## "The Eternal Within"

Just beyond this vision in the layers of purple ether,
Where the tops of the cloud fields gather light in their basins,
Where the rainbow threads of color tie together before our eyes,
And drape aloofly in glassy water shades,
Like water sky bands that soak the horizon,
It is there where this can only be found…

…Within.

## "Turn To You"

Flow throw me,
And make my waters still,
So that I may know,
The stillness for which You've intended;

I am frail,
Human, flesh,
I am steal,
And mortal,
I am forged in Your ultimate design,
Perfect in Your eyes,
Yet a gem in which I frequently see flaws;

This is as it is,
And perhaps as You have intended,
For if I saw no room to grow,
If I feared not,
And cried very little,
And laughed as a hint,
Then would I turn my eyes towards You…

…Oh Lord…

…I would like to believe that I would,
For You course through my frontier,
The big country with the big unending sky,
The artisan waterscape of light and love;

God, please cradle me in my sadness,
Please nurture my chest when next I fear,
Please warm me with Your smile,
When I grow tired, and weak, or despair;

Please hear me in my moments,
And share Your peace with me,
Please hold me, Lord, please hold me,
For I am asking for Your closeness here.

**"This Maven Ocean"**

Opal sparkles alight like a glaze,
Like silver blanket that rolls with the waves,
Dances on a turquoise sea that stretches out before me;

It crests and it dips in flickering display,
A million points of light at play,
This maven ocean's glitter waves crackle at my feet;

Maybe it, like this, a siren, behaves,
Because it knows no other way,
Pulling out from inside me my own eternal sea;

I breathe and feel the spray on my face,
And wear the silver blanket that lifts from the waves,
For who is yet the ocean - if he is not the sea.

**"In the Rising"**

Each pore sparkles across her angel skin,
Pouring out love that alights deeply from within,
She's got her hands outstretched,
And her hopes hinged,
Encouraging us in the channels that she finds,
Like tuning in a radio that scrambles into line;

I know my job, the challenge of man,
If I do not partake in the rising,
Then I cannot reach up to grab her hand,
And all I want to do is hold her hand -

Sparkling radiant diamonds that lead down a path towards you,
That doorway to the soul that shimmers,
In white bright crystalline red, green and blue…

…A million of love,
She is a million of love,
She watches us pass through each challenge,
Each grief,
Each pain,
Each gate,
With compassion in her voice,
And a smile on her face,
As my skiff simmers down in the calm,
As the sea flattens its face.

"The Flora of Exuma"

There are mangroves, Daddy, with opal shoots,
On the shallow, saline rich inlet side,
And Candlewood with petals of delicate flame,
Where the outcropped rocks pile jagged and high,
And wild palms like willows that bring a tear to your eye,
And Coco Plum and Sugar Apple and fragrant fruit trees,
With crystal leaves,
That reflect like diamonds when kissed by sunny sky;

I write poetry with you, Daddy, under the Yellow Elder,
Its bouquet of buttercups hint of our long talks,
Your voice in this breeze,
Dancing upon fresh green stalks,
With turquoise waters singing just beyond my feet;

And I paint ripe Sea Grapes dangling on thick cords,
That droop along the dune line,
And decorate this edge of the shore,
In red and purple and emerald lime,
That radiate as they breathe;

And I change the scenery, Daddy, whenever I wish,
Whenever I wave my hand with intention,
Whenever the mood takes me in another direction,
While I decorate our beach,
The flora here is lovely, Daddy,
It sings to me in an angel's speech,
And accentuates our home.

## "Soul Channel"

We reach upward into the depth of despair,
Fomenting internal conversation from the seedlings of fear,
And its mountains - hear the fountains groan,
Calling the waters downward into pools carved in stone,
Where we wash the dreams that lie dormant at our feet,
And slide beneath the spaces of our teeth,
As we drink the tears grown from its domain;

Morning finds the ocean curtailed by the tides,
Pushed upon the course as the moon decides,
And so the waters flow,
And flow and flow and flow,
And so as with these waters,
I've only to unclasp the mountains and let go,
And open up the channels to my soul.

**"An Extrasolar Super Earth (Supple In Her Hand)"**

A sun's flare sparks in the cornea of this artistic eye,
Something of which I always trust in her,
She has envisioned a perfect, scenic beach,
Upon an extrasolar super earth,
Draped with swaths of natural living light,
That emanate from the slow and deliberate...

...Waving of her hands;

Swirling auroras, deeply organic, tonal and bright,
Such blinding, stunning beauty,
Just as you are, My Love,
Psychedelic skies drenched with flowing spectral rainbows,
Rolling orange strobes,
Streaming through living water,
Spiking in the atmosphere like liquid glass,
And drifting back down in crystalline sheets of emerald rain,
Sink back into the seas,
Emitting a fresh, salty, sandy scented...

Air...

## "In the Glory of the Afterglow"

As crystal rash spread in water,
With a heated, humid, afterglow,
Illuminating ice green turquoise,
And clouds that spark of minty indigo,
It bled over coral, rocks and jagged shoals,
And spread in the crevasses,
Refracting as it grows,
Beaming in the sunlight,
Where shiny diamonds laugh and dance,
In the glory of the afterglow,
Spreads a luminous water rash.

**"Constant Joy"**

With the sun from your skin,
Flowing out from within,
With the moon in your eyes,
And a veil ever thin,
It is you for whom the sun wakes and glows;

And deep within each of your pores,
Galaxies open through each tiny door,
Where the worlds begin and overlap and end,
Nobody knows,
Except for those such as you,
With a universal view,
And an incorruptible soul;

With the sun in your skin,
Flowing out from within,
And the gold in your eye,
Like the moon in the sky,
You watch with active mind over your home;

We are all your embrace,
The smile on your face,
A constant joy that you bless our mornings with,
As we together live…

…Though you have left your human home…

…My Darling, we are your glory,
In which the morning sun glows.

**"Aqua Opal Seascape"**

Blanket of silver sparkles,
Blend with lemon crests of flaxen waves,
A hundred thousand points of light,
Spread out when ocean sprays,
Aqua opal seascape,
Its turquoise blues ingrained,
My aqua opal sea-dreams,
They wash away life's strains.

## "Floating Like Flowers on the Ocean"

Flowers of the ocean,
Petals pastel ink and scarlet green,
The calm waters reflect like a mirror,
Like floral stars sparkle in a dream,
The sky flows aquatic,
Awash in watery scene,
While the sea holds the pink clouds,
Like a blanket of steam;

The silver quilt of the moonlight,
Threads the sun's honey amber blades,
We watch the horizon evaporate,
And merge the night into day,
And deep within the mural,
Where the migraine finally released,
I found my elusive focus...

...Though I was now twenty paces deep;

I flow like flowers on the ocean,
Take me where the tide has run its course,
I surrender to the current and the swirling color,
And escape through another spirit door,
Floating closer and closer and closer,
I hear you calling me to your shore,
Ceili, you laugh in unconfined excitement,

"Daddy, keep coming...just a little further...just a little bit more..."

...I see you, Ceili, with sea oat blonde hair,
Shiny, golden and windswept,
Blowing in the breeze and glittering the air,
Your striking beauty, so pleasant, gentle and kind,
Only the blue of Exuma matches the blue of your eyes,
I reach for you, Daughter, my lovely, lovely child,
Please be patient with me, Sweetheart, on these last few miles...

...Of this current phase called a physical life...

**"Searching for Ceili Cay"**

The sun, it glows, it warms my tired face,
While sailing, cutting through a forest of white opal foam,
Through the aqua estuaries, and ancient sandbars,
On an open water poem,
Searching for uncharted terra firma,
That leaves salty, sweaty dust clinging to the skin,
I bank into the wind,
And in through prayer,
And jag at the sea,
On an ethereal journey toward Heaven...

...Searching for Ceili Cay...

...In the wilderness of the Out Islands,
Around the crystal shallows of the next shoal,
As an unknown land comes into view,
The ocean recedes into white sandy gold,
Turquoise water splashes on the keel,
Floating over big red starfish,
That linger on the face of the sea bottom field,
Where graceful gray wings of mighty ray glide,
And nurse sharks gather in the swollen tide,
Just aft of my eyes,
As my wooden hull scrapes forward into the soft sand and stops...

...And I have arrived...

# POSTCARDS FROM CEILI'S CAY

## "A Quiet Rain and the Quietude of Quilted Cloud"

A million droplets of rain,
Each itself with a trace,
Of you and your daytime moon;

As the warm showers, so gentle, so light,
Fall, they glisten of prayers, alight,
Each torched in a fire bloom...

...The smell of sweet rain on the salty air,
So quiet, you can only hear,
The breath of the wind,
And the dance of liquid beads on the leaves on the trees,
Tucked within the dunes.

**"Etheric Swarms of Higher Matter"**

Etheric centric and scented with life,
An astral companion on a channel of light,
She props up the road and prompts the doors open,
And propels the dimensions,
The ones we have chosen;

…Steam swarms in combustible air in a pre-determinate course,
Nor the light of radiation holds its truth above all external force…

…If light be transverse in its wave,
Could a miracle be explained away?
The spirit is itself breath,
That continues with the first inhale after death,
This body of stars that incarnate your elegant form,
An astral flesh stitched into an etheric mesh,
Unfolds as you were reborn;

Measurements of tangible aberration,
While the vital body, it lay upon the skin,
Radiating in an eternal aura,
This the doorway to the Eternal Light,
That expands and expounds across Exuma Infinite,
And washes the pain from these eyes.

## "The Mystic"

The Mystic in his spiritual pursuit,
Drinks the light from the Mangrove root,
Marks his heart, intended on a higher truth,
And absorption into the Absolute;

He finds the space beyond the eyes,
While the body, relaxed, it lies,
Tethered to his human skin,
While through dimensions his spirit flies;

And waters glow - far, far below,
Where rings of stars like oceans flow,
And turquoise suns illuminates a spirit road,
That converge in the endless center of the soul;

And through horizons and open doors,
And over mountains where timeless mornings glow,
He resonates in the Master's truth,
And blends into the Absolute.

**"Sleep in the Light (Of Your Soul)"**

Sleep, I may, in a spherical glow,
As I fall asleep in the fire of your soul,
Like resting in the furrows of the sun,
Where a seedling, dressed in this water halo light,
Will find its roots, its dreams…

…Its growth.

**"Uniola Paniculata"**

The Foredune grasses show us versatility,
We savor their resilience in this ability,
Conquering the erosive natural strains,
Sand blasting burials and stinging salt spray;

And flooding, drought, and low nutrients,
All challenge the sea oat of its opulence,
Yet with dense root systems and low profiles,
And high flower rates that stretch for miles,
They survive the pains and the stresses of the heart,
And thrive though the palm trees are ripped apart,
For when the hurricane, it roared and raged,
The roots, they never gave way or disengaged...

...And the sands remain though the beachfront change,
And the beach, itself, is rearranged,
Yet faith, it's face, built grain by grain,
Can never be completely wiped away...

...And as the howling winds turn to salty dust,
And as the humidity settles in the toiling musk,
The morning glory bloom in purple petal parades,
And wrap around the cord-grass where the sea oat strays.

**"A Circle of Lightning"**

Your love is electric,
It's radiance - the water wire of lightning,
That fires from cloud to cloud;

Your love is magnificence,
That leaves a constant impression,
And leaves no doubt;

You draw my name in the wind,
You press your light in my hand,
You carry your weary Father,
Like Footprints in the Sand;

Your love is courageous,
It weaves from life to life through life,
Your love is contagious,
Spreading, like sunrise washes the night;

You paint my heart in the breeze,
You rest your head against my head,
For you are in love with your Father,
In whose love there is no end.

## "If Only We May Hear"

Opportunities howling in the winds of turmoil,
Electricity in the cloud banks where the edges boil,
Sustenance in the heavy rains that blanket the fields,
For in their downpour our crops will find its yield,
These challenges are blessings that populate our path,
With God's tiny messages that lay just beyond our grasp;

I stood in the daylight in an ultraviolet silhouette,
With a smile on my lips my face cannot forget,
If in the beaming light,
Just perchance as nighttime flakes,
She penetrates, communicates, generates,
A light that Heaven gave;

Purple silk, thin ribbons, tree dressed,
Branches in the yard, confess,
Lanterns set the fires awake,
Like four vigilant stars,
We are,
Marking home in which the angel plays;

And neither the stars can be with no sky,
Just like the light of our lives blend,
Twined among your mother, your brother, you and I,
It breathes and it grows - a world without end.

**"Constant Vigilance"**

Defects they try to cling to my light,
Like dye crosses water with a dancing knife,
Defects they crawl and they peek around corners,
Sniffing for weakness along the borders,
These defects are defects and nothing more,
They can only harm me if I let them explore,
And so I remain vigilant at my soul's sacred door,
And process this light - and process some more...

...We breathe and our wind blows through the palms,
We breathe and our wind weaves into songs,
We breathe and our lives intertwine,
We breathe and your light lifts with mine,
Sitting with you, lovely Daughter,
Immersed in the tears of Atlantic's waters,
As I watch you walk into the sun.

## "She Talks To Me"

Water whisper - chasing bands of brilliant color in the ocean spray,
Raptures in collapse upon the beach in grand display,
The sea - she utters phrases in a spirit's dialect,
Often tonal enough for the ears to inspect,
If only we could shed the chains of our incessant humanity,
With its fragile crystal box of delicate sanity,
While the waves - in song and dance, crash into the conscience,
And breathe across our skin,
She talks to me,
In the rumble churned to silence…

As I walk with my daughter on a beach's sandy face.

**"Healing Light"**

Crystal river of effervescent light,
Its golden sparkling diamond flakes,
Run along the valleys,
And light up the basins with their lakes;

It flows within this country,
As long and deep as it is wise,
From the birth of an eternity,
Across heaven and its skies;

Its radiance is contagious,
Its warmth expands within its flow,
Once the waters of healing,
Have released within your soul;

And so stream crystal lightning channels,
That wipe away the wounding of the night,
Deeply within your journey,
Awaken healing light.

**"Fields of Cloud"**

The winds enliven the bones in the fields of clouds,
Green and lush landscape with its crushed velvet shrouds,
Brilliant emeralds captured in the grains of bitter rains,
Drawn from the channels that hold our Heaven's veins;

And the lashing tears that blow across the boiling sea,
Scorching the horizon in this smoky scene,
I cling to the notion like I would cling to my boat,
If I were lost to the ocean I'd hold onto to this hope;

That there always seems to be reason in this,
And through the storm somehow the sun's light persists,
Even if only along the fringes and dark edging,
Its mystic blessing alights life's most delicate threading,
Guiding us through the thick roiling fields of clouds,
And their luminous cross stitch and ethereal webbing,
Pressing our path with more purpose now…

…And pressing us in embrace as the dimensions align.

**"The Silver Glittering"**

Fire beads and silver bracelets woven with liquid stars,
Adorn her wrists with delicate, sparkling metals,
And accentuate the heart,
She with long white robes that glisten with the bands of silvery moon,
Drape the waves as they crest and break,
As they burst into foam and bloom...

...And swim, baby turtles, towards floral ocean dreams,
Beyond the swirling of the shallow surf,
To sargassum gardens where the ocean breathes;

They swim through silver glittery water,
Slide into your hands,
Cupped as cradles that comfort the sea,
They rest on your fingers and bare reverence to your peace,
That flows from your voice and your innocence.

**"On This Angelic Road..."**

In this human dimension the optics are limited,
Though not an optical illusion,
In the sky caps of higher dimension,
In the kaleidoscope of ascension,
Where the colors crash and blend and glow,
And this life can mimic an intrusion,
In the expanse of this astral tunnel,
Along the edges of angelic road,
I see the vestige of my lives flash and flow,
Like a living spark that illuminates a window,
And in this halo of allusion...

...I see my higher life.

**"The Linguistics of Death"**

Hush, the melody of music comes,
Our ears must sacred stand,
Our hearts may cherish opal fields,
With diamond flowers that sprout from land;

Yet words like barbs on prickly tongue,
The ignorance of man,
Proclaimed with little thought or effort,
Will clench the open hand;

Yet your miracles, like brilliant sun,
As in the morning comes,
For all to see - and with belief,
A new day has begun,
You are changing the manner in which the words are set,
You are ever changing the linguistics of death,
You are grinding down the barbs,
And nurturing the tongues,
Healing the ways we communicate,
Amongst each other…

…One to one to one…

**"Walking a Full Moon"**

The Full Moon huddled in the safety of painted, oily waves,
It's droplets of light scatter like fire jewels,
Sprinkling and dusting the tidal pools,
And the rolling fields of the shallows,
With silver flames,
And sparkle on the beachfront with misty water petals,
Where the moist sand absorbs the Moon's luminous blaze,
Softly sinking in the sand where our steps are traced,
Where we walk hand in hand,
In a sacred manner,
In this sacred place…

…You hand me a star that glowed in your hand,
And showed me how to flick the wrist just right,
Instructing your father in the nuances of life,
And I listen and I understand,
And I try, though I am still a man,
Skipping stars across the night sea…

…With each bounce the glitter bursts.

**"Owls We Are Of Night"**

We have always been owls on the night,
Awake, perched highly in passion,
Artistically experimenting with oils in the shadows,
And pencil shades,
Chalk on wood and oven stone,
And pastels in the rains,
Poetry brushstrokes,
And acrylic vibrant paint,
As the hours all huddle expended,
At the feet of our most lovely Saints;

We are of the night,
But not tucked within its darkness,
We are in the night,
The light of life that sparked this,
This brilliance in the bounty,
This power in the air,
This energy and spirit,
That drifts in twilight's atmosphere,
We are effortless with our eyes closed,
We are magnetic in the flow,
We are owls on the night,
From our perch atop the nightly pine…

…The ocean moon casts a silhouette of silence,
That makes a calming window,
Letting in a prism of tiny bands of light,
As the waves in the distance break,
Echo, tucked among the pinecones,
Quiet here…

…And wide, so wide awake.

**"Heaven Beach"**

It is where we go together...

...Surround me,
Blow like lively wind through my soul,
And lift me to a higher vibration,
Take me to our Heaven Beach,
With its dark purple sky and golden stars,
With its turquoise waters and rolling white sands,
Where we walk its contours,
Together, hand in hand;

...You are now wearing black shorts and an off white top,
An outfit I see you in frequently,
In my meditation,
Your long golden hair blows in the breeze,
Your ancient blue eyes smile on your father,
As you prompt me to follow,
As you lead me down the contours,
Of our Heaven Beach.

**"A Blanket of Light"**

A textured mosaic of rugged humanity,
A thousand weak strings tighten firmly into rope,
We shed our wishes, our failures, our searching,
We shelve ourselves in search of hope;

Once smoky trails of deadened embers,
Pathetic paths marking the remains of our souls,
We strike out, wailing, with obsession prevailing,
We cling in the beginning with a threadbare hold;

We wrap ourselves in this blanket of light,
We breathe into its mystic terrain,
We sing its gift in the faces that reflect us,
For in this interlocking - this fabric remains.

**"I Still Believe"**

When, in this life, and in this cruelty,
In this inequity, unfair and burden blind,
When, to a good family, tragedy comes,
The foundation may be destroyed,
The foundation may crumble in the void -

But not I, oh Lord,
Not I...

When, should the life obliterate before us,
Should the dreams explode into sharp shards of dust,
Should the hopes and plans and effortlessness,
Evaporate,
If the soul be eviscerated, what truth do we hold true,
In the crux of this cruelly spiked vein,
What shall the righteous do,
Oh, what shall the righteous do?

Still, I believe,
Through the window of grief,
I still believe,
In the shadow of this massive thief,
I still believe,
In the vacuum where the tempest seethes,
I still believe,
My child...

...Walking the sands of Ceili Cay,
Walking here beside me...

...It is the higher truth,
Here by this turquoise sea,
It is me and you...

...I still believe.

**"Visible Light"**

Tucked within the infrared and ultraviolet, succumbed,
Packed into our little lives, limited and spirit numb,
Lives the lovely burden of visible light,
All that we believe in, derived from human sight;

Where perhaps a hint of high blue can be seen as an infant,
Our eyes soon dull into the fanciful lens of self-centered human consumption,
Leading us astray from our spirit,
The one eye conceived of truth...

...Though the channel be obscured,
It is never truly severed in the process,
Yet this, unknown, for most who grope the air blindly,
Remains a hidden path to abundance...

...Visible light is light but little,
A mirage signaling oasis in the distance,
Spluttering waves of mistruth,
Into the hulking deception of bitter time,
A keyhole in through which life is viewed,
Limited, listless, lifeless, misconstrued...

...And all along the perimeter,
Fabricated metal fences of flesh,
Act as a barrier to the eyes,
An unnatural enterprise,
That some have found quite comforting,
And others found unwise...

...Can you tell me where the lamb, astray, has been found,
Returned to its pastures in a paradise of a Higher Ground...

## "Inflorescence"

Four sweet flowers, a clustered bloom,
Four sweet spirits - four interlaced moons,
Four together, tethered, windblown and groomed,
Four that form one whole,
These souls, they root into eternal dunes,
The sand of which may shift,
The form of which may drift,
Yet never is the heart of this exhumed;

Ocean flowers of Exuma are we,
Clustered as a family,
An ornate arrangement,
Morphologically,
Four cords of light,
Spiritually,
That never the earth may pull apart,
Four interlaced moons fleshed in one heart,
Flowing upon the aqua waves…

…Of an endless sea…

**"Salt Water Taffy"**

We track down the beach with our feet sinking in magical sands,
As you convey as much wisdom to me,
As I can understand,
And under our feet,
The powder like pastel fluorescent salt water taffy,
We are here, on the edges of two dimensions,
Egging each other on,
And laughing,
As the doors of heaven swing in the breeze,
An open ocean not made of dreams,
But fleshed in the sugar strands of this life.

### "Green Water"

The thunder rash of afternoon has left behind its heated smoky robes,
They lay upon the waters,
Half-moon, soon to sip the night soup of thickly humid cloaks,
Hanging over the vestal seascape,
Where the pixies and the angels and the trumpeters of Heaven...

...Emerge with their jovial songs.

**"Liquid Dreams"**

Her arms drape across stellar indigo fields,
Gowns of wedding midnight white,
Leaving their colorful marks,
Like one million shooting stars scratch across the night,
Spiritually habitable,
Spiritually audible,
Spiritually palpable,
Spiritually alive;

"For all, from one," she cries out in joyous release,
The message of this angel in the credo of peace,
Active, alive, wise and mystic,
She waves her hands to disperse the vapor that lingers in tidal pulls,
That swirl with sound and light,
Liquid and rhythmic,
A silvery glow, like glittery sparks from her fingers ignite,
And fill the purple evening with a field of green stars…

…Morpheus swims here in a delicate flavor,
While she harvests jewels from her birthstone that incubate life,
Crushing the emerald stones into liquid dream,
While he lay, slumber traveler, wrapped in sleepy dominion,
She passes him oceans of aquamarine,
And draws his ragged skiff,
That has drifted in the surf,
Back to the beach of Ceili Cay…

…Once again…

### "Daddy, Thank You for Your Miracles"

"Daddy, I love the strength we exhibit in focusing on reconciliation, rather than chasing the tail of what society says is 'healing.' Most people won't understand this. You're not supposed to 'heal,' not the way society thinks someone heals. Not with the physical passing of a child. Healing is the wrong target. The wrong expectation society places on people - you see judgmental people all over the place, most of whom have not physically lost a child. Feeling the grief and walking through it whenever the waves arise, and reconciling it, this is the right target. The right expectation.

You know the duality - the daily losses that truly accumulate and the grief - that is reality - it is unavoidable - and the daily counterbalance of blessings and the joy in our relationship - that is also reality. It co-exists, one with the other, in an ever dancing array of emotion within the moments that construct our lives. As it should be.

You already know to feel grief does not mean you have failed; that there is not something wrong with your spiritual condition. If anything you are the contrary. You don't fall apart and lay on the ground and destroy your life in despair after my accident. You don't dishonor me like that. You don't leave the destruction of your life upon my shoulders.

You walk through the grief like a badass with courage. You walk through the first truth of my tragic physical death and embrace life as much as you can in our family of four. But by embracing life it doesn't mean you don't grieve. You do both. You have sadness and happiness, grief and joy, suffocating torture and miracles at my fingertips. As it should be.

You see, we are bigger than our physical bodies. And regardless of our physical lives, we are always together. I am here. Presently. Currently. Not in your heart. Not in your thoughts. You don't keep me alive. You don't keep my memory alive. I am here all by myself. Living right now, with you or without you thinking about me or feeling me, even though I know you think about me and feel me all day long!

I am alive in this elevated body. And you know it. And that is your miracle, Daddy. That is the miracle you give me as we interact each day and continue to develop our relationship. How humbled am I that you think I give out all the miracles, when in fact, I also receive miracles from my Daddy - daily. Keep walking. Keep co-existing. Keep balancing the first truth and the second truth. Keep reconciling. Keep the expectation where it should be. Keep your side of our relationship growing and I will do the same. I am so proud of you, Daddy. Thank you for your miracles."

## "The Golden Road"

Breathe with these eyes,
Feel with this soul,
Hear with my essence,
While I see...

...With my trusting eyes closed,
For my eyes lift awakened,
To the unfolding of the Golden Road,
It lay over the waters that blanket the sea,
That expand into path over waves,
Planked by water beams,
That breathe of the ocean,
That breathe through my feet,
That stream through my soul...

...For we know,
We are not of this world,
Nor is the bridge of this liquid road,
We are not of the flesh,
Nor the body caged in bone,
We are of spirit,
Of which to behold...

...As my heart sings your name,
As I walk Golden Road.

**"And Lengths Across These Waves"**

The distance between successive crests,
Tolls the length of this wave,
Whether electric, spiritual or sound,
It is itself a universe within its range,
A channel of communication,
A frequency of light,
Thought we face the turbulence of charging tides,
And variant shapes and sizes of the waves,
At the core of grief…

…All waves and all light similarly behave.

**"Ceili Cay, Exuma"**

Neon salt crystals in minty sea, radiate,
In these shallows, water lightning combusts and illuminates,
Like the sun was captured under the waves,
Like the sun is buried in the sand as bright as a summer day,
While this streak of living light, like a heartbeat, strobes,
And pulses and refracts in a web of water gold...

...That dances in the laughter of her feet.

## "It Is…"

It is here,
It is now,
It is in Cleveland,
And here in the cays,
Blending somehow,
It is the physical,
It is the spirit world,
It is eternity,
It is avowed,
It is God's grace,
Which He Himself allows,
It is the future,
And lives in the past,
And into the moment,
These dimensions collapse,
For it is you,
And it is me,
It is here in Exuma,
On the edge of aqua sea,
It is the promise of perfect peace…

…This is the light,
Sitting here together,
On our pristine beach,
Contemplating new life and our golden dreams,
Watching the seabirds…

…Swimming through stars fields,
Lying your head on my shoulder…

…Where your soul finds its seat…

**"The Cay of Life"**

A lifeblood that resonates,
It vibrates through each grain of sand,
Like the cells and veins and bones,
That flesh the organism of man;

It breathes upon its own accord,
It's movements in this changing shore,
Its heartbeat pulses of living water,
And living dunes…

…A land we call "Freedom,"
In the tangle of the Exuma Cays,
A temple constructed with the melody,
Of the vigilant trumpets of angels,
That crowd in the skies,
To wrap us in the comfort of their quilted wings...

…That never fail the faithful eye.

www.ingramcontent.com/pod-product-compliance
Lightning Source LLC
Chambersburg PA
CBHW011140290426
44108CB00020B/2698